HOW TO READ A COMIC BOOK

Comic books are made up of pictures in boxes, called panels. Look at each of these panels from left to right, and top to bottom.

Read the speech bubbles, caption boxes and any sound effects from left to right, too. Together with the images, these will tell you the story.

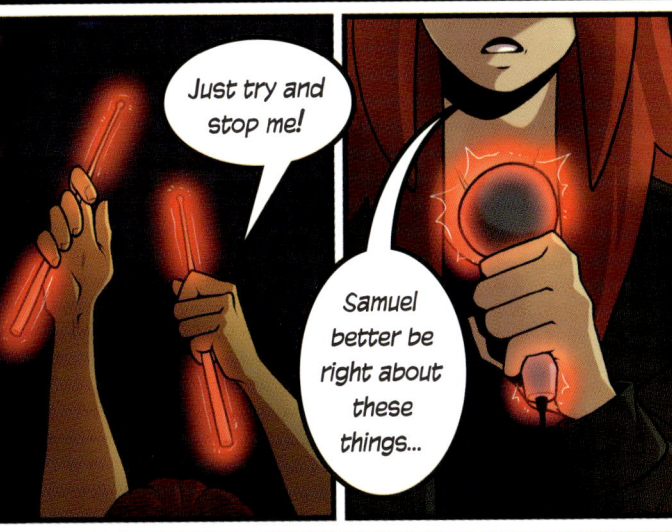

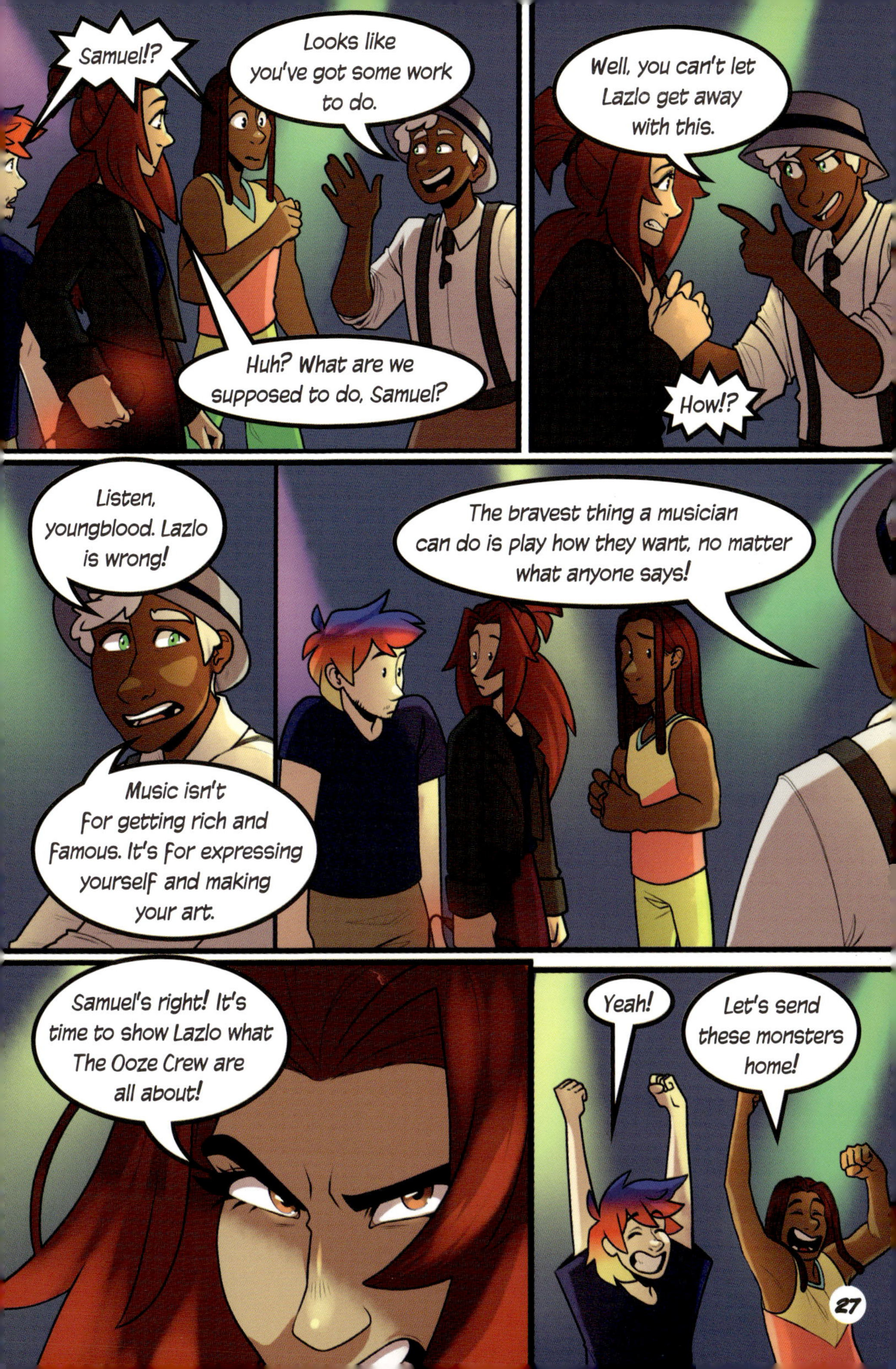

@2024 BookLife Publishing Ltd.
King's Lynn, Norfolk, PE30 4LS, UK

ISBN 978-1-80505-289-0

All rights reserved. Printed in India.
A catalogue record for this book is
available from the British Library.

The Ooze Crew
Written by Noah Leatherland
Illustrated by T Morrell

ABOUT BOOKLIFE GRAPHIC READERS

BookLife Graphic Readers are designed to encourage reluctant readers to take the next step in their reading adventure. These books are a perfect accompaniment to the BookLife Readers phonics scheme and are designed to be read by children who have a good grasp on reading but are reluctant to pick up a full-prose book. Graphic Readers combine graphic and prose storytelling in a way that aids comprehension and presents a more accessible reading experience for reluctant readers and lovers of comic books.

ABOUT THE AUTHOR

Noah is a lifelong fan of comic books, video games, movies and pro wrestling. Trying to tap into all the things that make these hobbies cool is what drives Noah's writing. Noah was a reluctant reader as a kid (and still is), so he hopes to put a bit more fun and excitement into children's books.

ABOUT THE ILLUSTRATOR

T has been an artist since they were 11 years old, dreaming of being able to bring stories to life. T has become an artist of all trades, learning everything they can to follow their dream. T's passion for art has led them to working on video games, costumes, and now comic books!